2ND EDITION

T

LEVEL 2A

MW00979997

PIANO
Adventures®

by Nancy and Randall Faber

THE BASIC PIANO METHOD

Thanks and acknowledgement to Victoria McArthur
for her collaboration on the First Edition of this book.

FABER
PIANO ADVENTURES®
3042 Creek Drive
Ann Arbor, Michigan 48108

8th Notes

run - ning   walk

=   **1 count or beat**

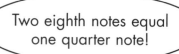

Two eighth notes equal
one quarter note!

Create 8th Note Patterns!

1.
- Draw a **quarter note** above the word "walk."
- Draw **eighth notes** above the word "run-ning." Hint: Draw a "house" ⌐⌐ , then the noteheads.
- Tap your rhythms, saying the words aloud.

Ex.

a. 4/4

walk   run - ning   walk   run - ning   walk   run - ning   walk   walk

b. 4/4

run - ning   walk   run - ning   walk   run - ning   walk   walk   walk

c. 4/4

run - ning   run - ning   walk   walk   run - ning run - ning   walk   walk

2.
- Draw a bar line after every *4 counts*.
- Draw a double bar line at the end (thin line, thick line).
- Can you write **1 2 3 4** under the correct notes?

Famous Rhymes with 8th Notes

1.
   - Say each Famous Rhyme aloud. Feel its natural rhythm.
   - Next, **tap** the Famous Rhyme as you say the words.
   - Now draw a line from each Famous Rhyme to the rhythm that matches.

2. Now copy **each rhythm** with your pencil. (Write it above each color box.)

Fiddle to My 8th Notes

1. Draw only **one note** in the blank violin to equal the **8th notes** of the first violin.

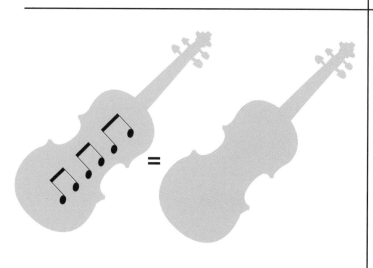 

2. Each fiddler's rhythm below is incomplete.

• Complete each measure with ONLY pairs of **8th notes**.

Ex.

a.

b.

c.

Lesson p.12 (Skip to My Lou)   FF108

The Natural ♮

A natural cancels a sharp or flat. A natural will **always be a white key**.

The Popcorn Bowl

1.
 • Circle each **natural** ♮ in the music below.
 • Now sightread the melody.

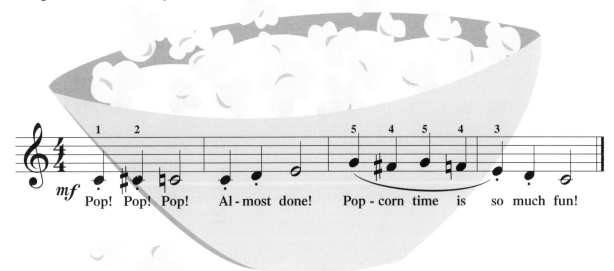

mf
Pop! Pop! Pop! Al - most done! Pop - corn time is so much fun!

2. Put a ✓ on the correct key to match each popcorn kernel below.

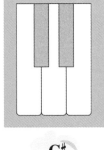

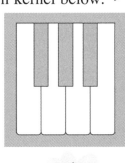

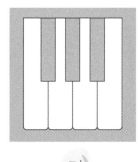

C♯   C♮   B♭   B♮

3. A natural can be on a **line** or in a **space**.

 • Trace these naturals.
   Hint: Draw an "L," then a "7."

4.
 • Trace each natural. Then draw another natural beside the one you traced.

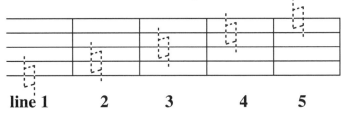

line 1   2   3   4   5

 • Trace each natural. Then draw another natural beside the one you traced.

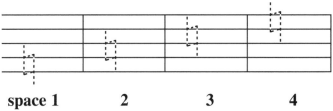

space 1   2   3   4

Though Bach's music is over 250 years old, it has influenced all kinds of music—from choir music to pop sounds of today.

Here, Bach's minuet is changed into a "pop" song.

- Add bar lines after every **4 beats**.
  Notice the time signature changed from $\frac{3}{4}$ to $\frac{4}{4}$.

- Write 1 - 2 - 3 - 4 for the correct beats in *measures 1-7*.

- Play with the teacher duet.
  Which version of Bach's melody do you like the best?

A Jazzy Song for Mr. Bach

from the Notebook for Anna Magdalena Bach
arranged by Nancy Faber

Cheerfully

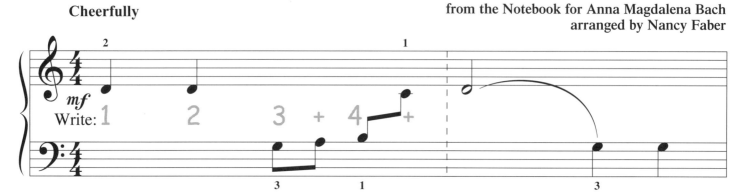

Write: 1   2   3   +   4   +

Teacher Duet: (Student plays *1 octave higher*)

Did you know...
Bach was orphaned at age 9.

Bach walked over 200 miles to hear an organ concert.

Bach composed over 1000 works in his lifetime.

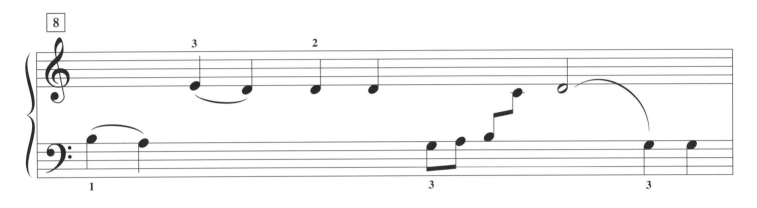

Your teacher will play Bach's melody in $\frac{3}{4}$ or $\frac{4}{4}$ time.
Listen carefully and name the **time signature**!
Do this several times.

7

Brahms loved to read and eventually had over 800 books as an adult!

Brahms became so famous, he is now known as one of the 3 B's — Bach, Beethoven, and Brahms!

Mr. Brahms' Time Signature Game

1. Write $\frac{3}{4}$ or $\frac{4}{4}$ before each measure of rhythm.

2. Now write 1 2 3 or 1 2 3 4 under the correct notes.

Brahms loved gypsy bands. Gypsy melodies and rhythms inspired his music.

Brahms wrote 4 symphonies that are among the greatest in orchestra music.

Brahms is buried beside Beethoven.

- Write in each **time signature**.
- Clap the rhythm with your teacher.
- Set a steady beat and sightread.

Gypsy Tunes!

Briskly

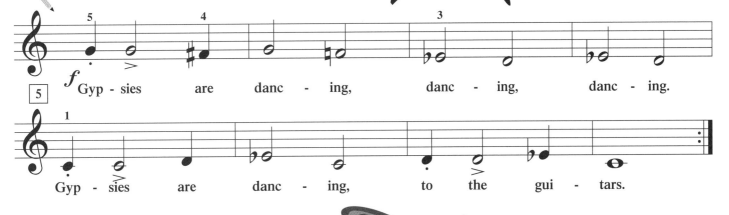

f Gyp - sies   are   danc - ing,   danc - ing,   danc - ing.

Gyp - sies   are   danc - ing,   to   the   gui - tars.

Moderately
(run-ning run-ning walk)

mf

Your teacher will play example **a** or **b**.
Listen carefully and circle the correct example.

LISTEN...

1a.

or

b.

2a.

or

b.

3a.

or

b.

4a.

or

b.

Transposing

Transposing means playing the same music using a different scale.
The starting note will change but the **intervals** remain the same.

* Play these examples:

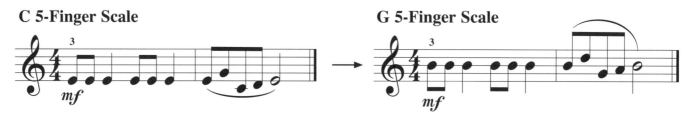

C 5-Finger Scale **G 5-Finger Scale**

Is Mr. Haydn Transposing?

1.
* Name each **interval** marked for the manuscript on the left—**2nd, 3rd, 4th, 5th**.
* Then circle the correct transposition on the right.

Surprise Symphony Theme

London Trio in G

Concerto in C

2. Knowing **intervals** will help you to transpose.

- Write the whole note to complete the interval on the staff.
- Then name both notes in the blanks.

Have fun reading about Mr. Haydn!

A Short Story about Mr. Haydn

 up a 4th    up a 2nd

H __ y __ n   lived over two   hun __ r __ d   fifty

 up a 4th    up a 3rd    up a 4th

y __ __ rs   ago.   His mother was a cook.   His __ __ ther   m __ __ e

 down a 2nd       down a 3rd    down a 5th

w __ __ ons.   At a __ __ __ six,   H __ y __ n   was sent to study music with a

 down a 4th   down a 2nd    down a 2nd    down a 5th

rel __ tiv __.   Later, he   s __ n __   and studi __ __   at the cathedral with his __ roth __ r.

 down a 3rd   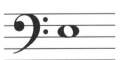 up a 4th    up a 3rd

As an adult, Haydn   be __ __ me a   musical   s __ rv __ nt   to a   prin __ __   in a

 up a 4th   up a 5th 

Haydn wrote 104 symphonies!

__ __ autiful   p __ lac __ .

Complete the information for each of Haydn's themes.

Mr. Haydn's Themes to Transpose

1. a. Name the **intervals** in the boxes.
   b. Play as written.
   c. Transpose to the **G 5-finger scale.**

from Symphony No. 100

Ex. | 2nd | 3rd

2. a. Name the **intervals** in the boxes.
   b. Play as written.
   c. Transpose to the **C 5-finger scale.**

from Symphony No. 104

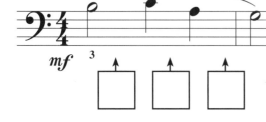

3. a. Name the **intervals** in the boxes.
   b. Play as written.
   c. Transpose to the **G 5-finger scale.**

from Symphony No. 30

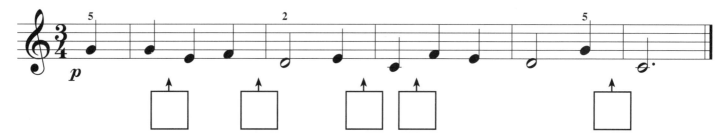

Listen to Bach, Beethoven, and Brahms

- Close your eyes and listen.
  Your teacher will play a short melody by Bach, Beethoven, or Brahms.

- Then your teacher will play a **transposed melody**. The transposed melody will be the **same** (correctly transposed) or **different** (incorrectly transposed).

- Circle same or different for the second pattern you hear.

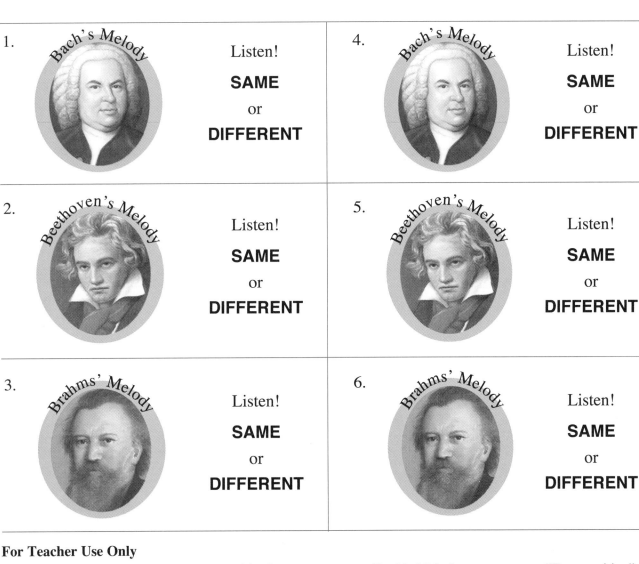

1. Bach's Melody — Listen! **SAME** or **DIFFERENT**

2. Beethoven's Melody — Listen! **SAME** or **DIFFERENT**

3. Brahms' Melody — Listen! **SAME** or **DIFFERENT**

4. Bach's Melody — Listen! **SAME** or **DIFFERENT**

5. Beethoven's Melody — Listen! **SAME** or **DIFFERENT**

6. Brahms' Melody — Listen! **SAME** or **DIFFERENT**

For Teacher Use Only

Crescendo and Diminuendo
(cres-SHEN-do)   **(di-min-u-EN-do)**

- Practice pointing to the words and pronouncing them aloud.

crescendo (cresc.)   *diminuendo (dim.)*

gradually louder   gradually softer

- Draw a ⟨ or ⟩ under each picture to show how it would sound.

the bugle boys coming closer

Draw:

a horse-drawn carriage riding away

Draw:

a boxcar disappearing in the night

Draw:

a traffic jam building up

Draw:

a helicopter landing in front of your house

Draw:

a kite drifting away in the wind

Draw:

Sightread these melodies. Watch for the *cresc.* and *dim.* markings.

Then transpose each to the 5-finger scale suggested.

Transpose to the **G 5-finger scale**.

The Elf's Little Train Set

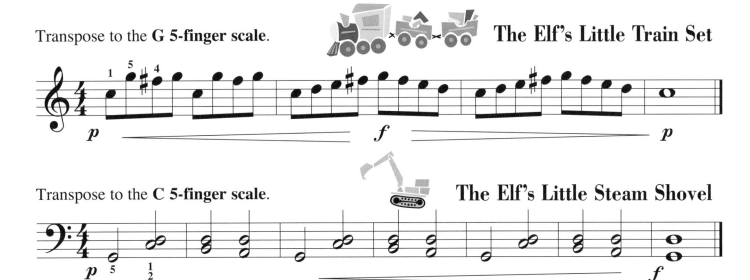

Transpose to the **C 5-finger scale**.

The Elf's Little Steam Shovel

Your teacher will play a musical example.

Circle *crescendo*, *diminuendo*, or both *cresc.* and *dim.* for what you hear.

1. *crescendo*

   diminuendo

   cresc. and *dim.*

2.

   < and >

3. *cresc.*

   dim.

   cresc. and *dim.*

4. *crescendo*

   diminuendo

   cresc. and *dim.*

5. *cresc.*

   dim.

   cresc. and *dim.*

6.

   < and >

For Teacher Use Only: The examples may be played in any order.

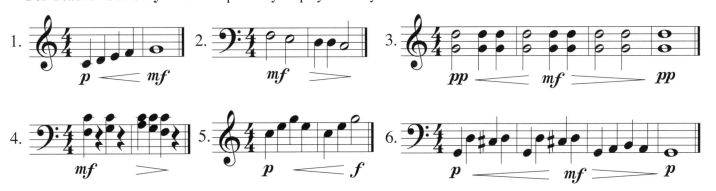

1. p < mf

2. mf >

3. pp < mf > pp

4. mf >

5. p < f

6. p ——— mf > p

The Phrase

A **phrase** is a musical sentence or idea. It usually is shown by a **phrase mark**.
A phrase mark looks the same as a *slur*.

phrase mark

Play and say: She sells sea shells by the sea - shore.

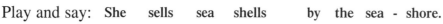

1.
• Say each tongue twister aloud three times for fun.
• In the music, write the time signature, **2/4**, **3/4**, or **4/4**.
• Draw phrase marks. Then play!

a. **Tongue Twister: Two toads totally tired.**

Notice how the musical phrase makes it easy to say!

time signature

Two toads to - tal - ly tir - ed.

b. **Tongue Twister: Friendly Fred flips fine flapjacks.**

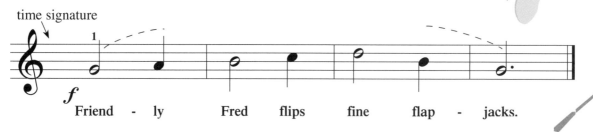

time signature

Friend - ly Fred flips fine flap - jacks.

c. **Tongue Twister:** **Big black bug bit a big black bear.**

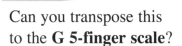

time signature

p Big black bug bit a big black bear.

Can you transpose this to the **G 5-finger scale**?

d. **Tongue Twister:** **Fred fed Ted bread and Ted fed Fred bread.**

time signature

mf Fred fed Ted bread and Ted fed Fred bread.

Can you transpose this to the **C 5-finger scale**?

Look out for this one!

e. **Tongue Twister:** **A skunk sat on a stump and thought the stump stunk, but the stump thunk the skunk stunk!**

Turn it into a musical phrase!

time signature

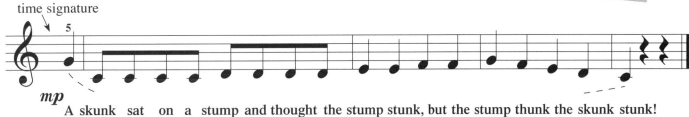

mp A skunk sat on a stump and thought the stump stunk, but the stump thunk the skunk stunk!

2. **Tongue Twister:** **Peter Piper picked a peck of pickled peppers.**

Can you make up your own melody for the words?

Two Interesting Facts about Phrases

Fact 1

Most piano music does NOT have words that point out the musical phrases.

Fact 2

Some music is composed of phrases, but phrase marks are NOT included in the music.

I Am the Phrase Finder!

- Draw a whole rest in each empty measure. (There are 9.)
- Draw **phrase marks** in the music to show each "musical sentence."
- Sightread the music and listen for the **phrases**.

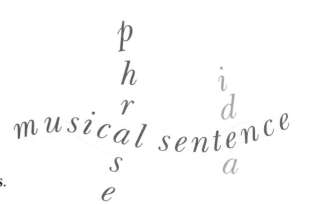

To end, repeat **measures 1-8.**

You Can Compose!

C 5-Finger Scale

L.H. 𝄢 5 4 3 2 1

C 5-Finger Scale

R.H. 𝄞 1 2 3 4 5

- Complete this piece by choosing notes from the **C 5-finger scale**.
  Use the rhythm given above each measure.

- Then draw phrase marks and dynamic markings (*p* , *mp* , *mf* , *f*).
  Play your composition!

If You Meet an Alligator

Words by Crystal Bowman

rhythm:

R.H.

dynamic marking ___

If you meet an al - li - ga - tor, bet - ter run and let him be!

5

L.H.

Do not greet or try to calm him with a moon-light mel - o - dy.

9

R.H.

dynamic marking ___

But if you should find a bun - ny or a kit - ten or a mouse,

13

L.H.

You may pet it ver - y gen - tly, then bring it in - to your house!

Half Step Review

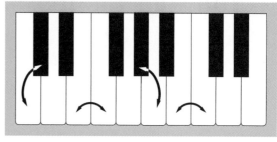

A **half step** is from one key to the *very next key*.

Playful Puppets

- Complete the half step challenge for each puppet.

What is a half step UP from E?

_____
answer

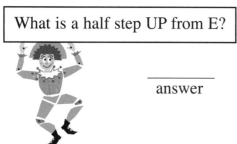

Draw a 𝅝 a half step LOWER.
Do you need a ♯ or ♭?

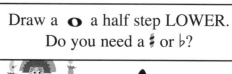

(you draw)

Circle the half steps. (There are 3.)

What is a half step DOWN from
A? Do you need a ♯ or ♭?

_____
answer

Draw a 𝅝 a half step LOWER.
Do you need a ♯ or ♭?

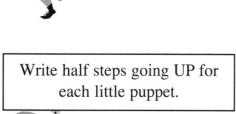

Circle the half step.

or

Write half steps going UP for
each little puppet.

going higher

Did you
land on G?

| C | C♯ | | | | | | |

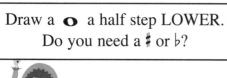

📖 Lesson p.28 (The Puppet Show)

FF1082

Whole Steps

A **whole step** is made up of 2 half steps.
Think of two keys with one key in between.

Detective "Whole Step"

1. Put a ✓ on the key a **whole step higher** than the keys with an X.

Ex.   Think!

2. Put a ✓ on the key a **whole step lower** than the keys with an X.

3. Draw a **whole step higher** than the notes given. Use a ♯ or ♭ as needed.

4.

Draw a **whole step lower** than the notes given. Use a ♯ or ♭ as needed.

Remember, to **improvise** means to create "on the spot."

Improvise "moon shadow" music by doing the following:

- First, listen to your teacher play the accompaniment.
  Feel the mysterious mood.

- When you are ready, play notes from this whole step pattern IN ANY ORDER.

- End by softly, playing all the R.H. keys together.

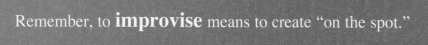

Moon Shadows Improv

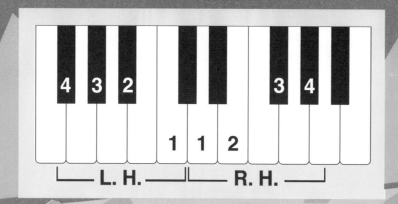

Did you know that Mars has two moons?

Teacher Improv Accompaniment: (Student improvises higher on the keyboard)
Moderately, mysteriously

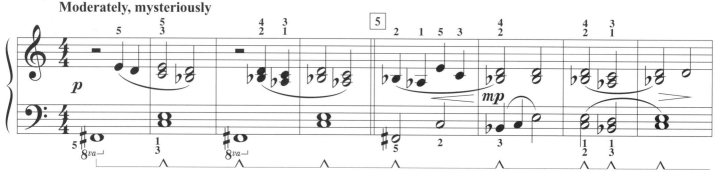

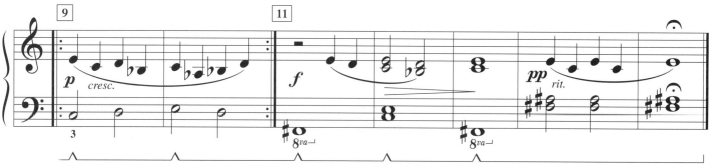

Draw a line connecting each
planet to its correct moon.

Planets and Moons

PLANET

whole
steps

half
steps

whole
and half
steps

PLANET

**a whole
step UP
from B♭**

PLANET

whole
and half
steps

whole
steps

half
steps

Your teacher will play either example **a** or **b**.

Listen carefully and circle the correct example.

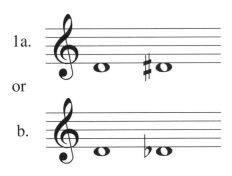

1a.

or

b.

2a.

or

b.

3a.

or

b.

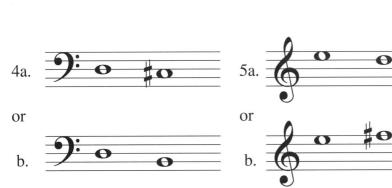

4a.

or

b.

5a.

or

b.

6a.

or

b.

Lesson p.32 (Storms on Saturn)

Cheers for the D Scale

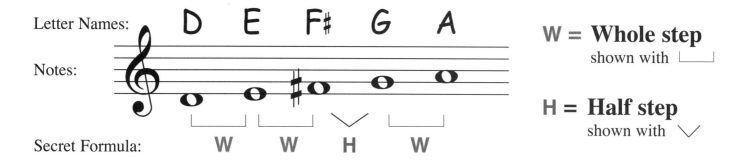

Letter Names: D E F♯ G A

Notes:

Secret Formula: W W H W

W = **Whole step**
shown with ⌐⌐

H = **Half step**
shown with ∨

1. • For each staff, complete the letter names for the **D 5-finger scale** in the blanks.
   • Next, write the missing whole notes on the staff.

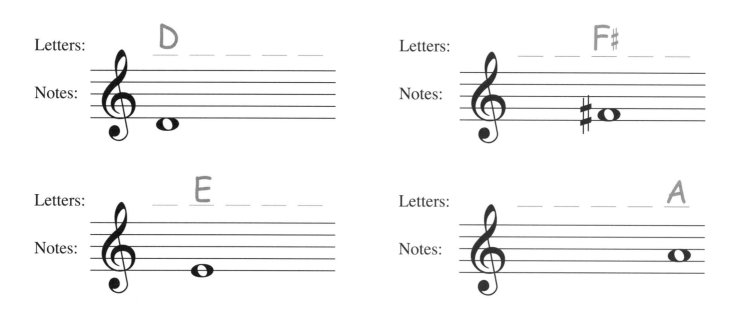

Letters: D _ _ _ _

Notes:

Letters: _ _ _ _ F♯

Notes:

Letters: _ E _ _ _

Notes:

Letters: _ _ _ _ A

Notes:

• Try the bass clef!

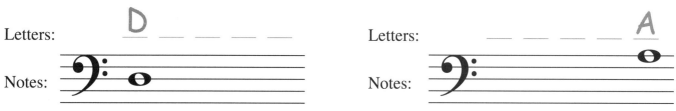

Letters: D _ _ _ _

Notes:

Letters: _ _ _ _ A

Notes:

2. For each scale above, mark the **whole steps** with a bracket ⌐⌐ and **half steps** with a wedge ∨.
   (See the top of the page.)

The D Chord -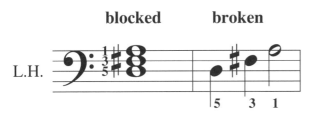

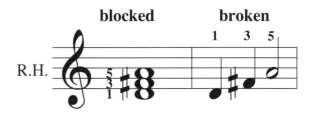

This Old Man Played This Old Chord

- Complete these challenges and review the chords you have learned: C, G, and D.

Write a **D blocked** chord.

Did you remember the #?

Name this **blocked** chord.

_____ chord

Write a **D broken** chord.

Did you remember the #?

Name this **broken** chord.

_____ chord

Write a **C blocked** chord.

Name this **broken** chord.

_____ chord

Name this **blocked** chord.

_____ chord

Name this **broken** chord.

_____ chord

Write a **G blocked** chord.

Name this **blocked** chord.

_____ chord

Write a **C blocked** chord.

Name these **blocked** chords.

chords: ___ ___ ___

1. • Write a whole note to complete the **interval**. ✏
   • Then name both notes in the blanks.
2. Have fun reading about Vivaldi!

A Short Story about Antonio Vivaldi

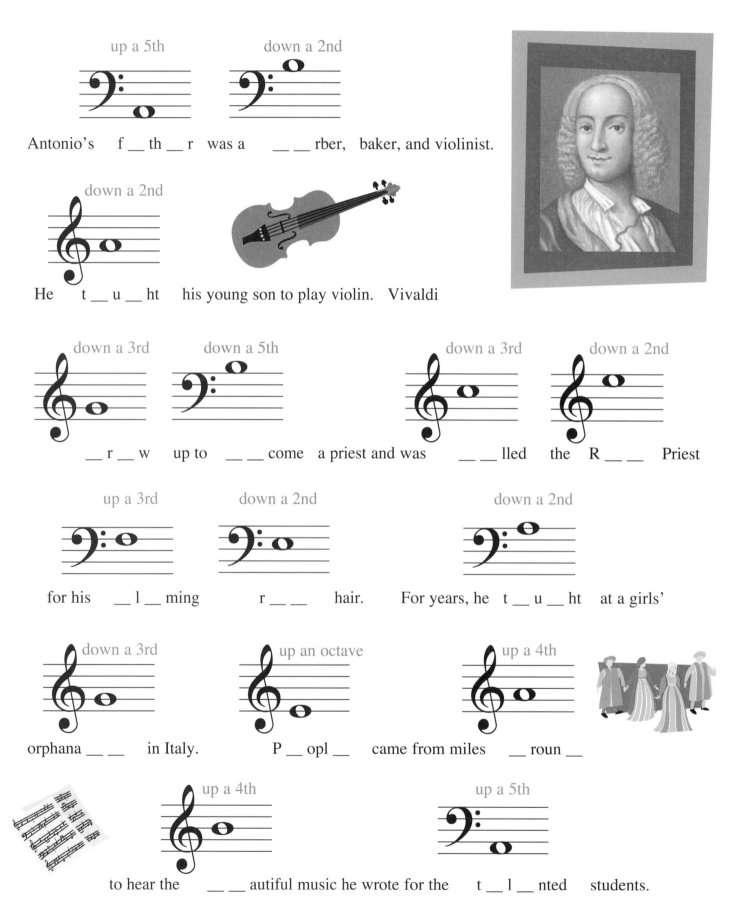

up a 5th   down a 2nd

Antonio's   f __ th __ r   was a   __ __ rber,   baker, and violinist.

down a 2nd

He   t __ u __ ht   his young son to play violin.   Vivaldi

down a 3rd   down a 5th   down a 3rd   down a 2nd

__ r __ w   up to   __ __ come   a priest and was   __ __ lled   the   R __ __   Priest

up a 3rd   down a 2nd   down a 2nd

for his   __ l __ ming   r __ __   hair.   For years, he   t __ u __ ht   at a girls'

down a 3rd   up an octave   up a 4th

orphana __ __   in Italy.   P __ opl __   came from miles   __ roun __

up a 4th   up a 5th

to hear the   __ __ autiful music he wrote for the   t __ l __ nted   students.

Vivaldi wrote over 500 concertos!
A concerto is a piece for one or more instruments accompanied by an orchestra.

Rhythm Trouble!

Many measures below are incorrect.

Draw an X through each measure with **incorrect rhythm**.
Hint: Look at the time signature.

a.

b.

c.

Your teacher will play either example **a** or **b**.

Listen carefully and circle the correct example.

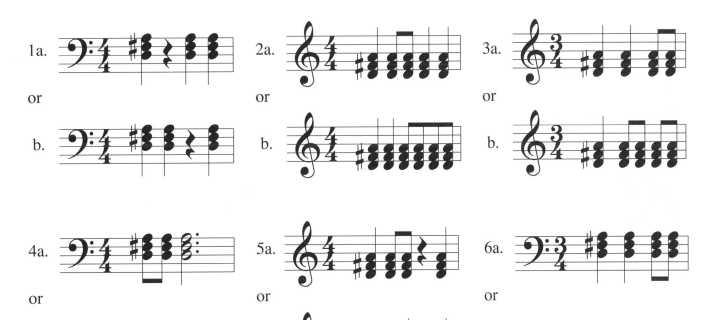

- Now YOU be the teacher. Play either example **a** or **b** to challenge your teacher.
  Be sure to use the correct hand.

Cheers for the  A Scale

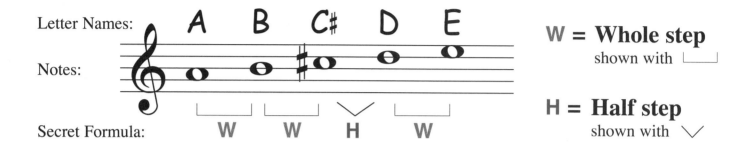

Letter Names: A B C♯ D E

Notes:

Secret Formula: W W H W

W = Whole step
shown with ⌐⌐

H = Half step
shown with ∨

1.
* For each staff, complete the letter names for the **A 5-finger scale** on the blanks.
* Next, write the missing whole notes on the staff.

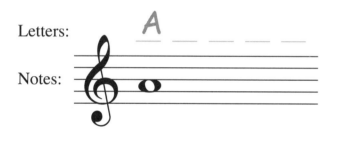

Letters: A _ _ _ _

Notes:

Letters: _ _ C♯ _ _

Notes:

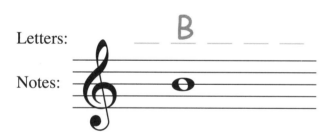

Letters: _ B _ _ _

Notes:

Letters: _ _ _ _ E

Notes:

* Try the bass clef!

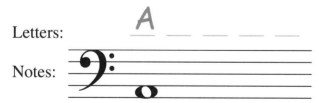

Letters: A _ _ _ _

Notes:

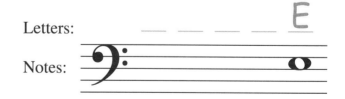

Letters: _ _ _ _ E

Notes:

2. For each scale above, mark the **whole steps** with a bracket ⌐⌐ and **half steps** with a wedge ∨.
(See the top of the page.)

The A Chord -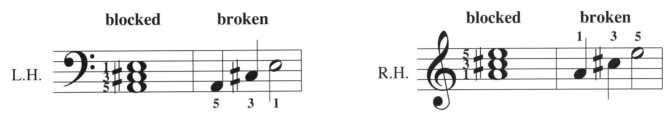

Peter Pan's Key Flight

- Name the scales and chords that Peter Pan sees on his flight.

_____ chord

_____ scale

_____ scale

_____ scale

_____ chord

_____ chord

_____ scale

_____ chord

_____ chord

_____ chord

_____ scale

_____ chord

_____ chord

Lesson p.43 (Peter Pan's Flight)

Questions and Answers

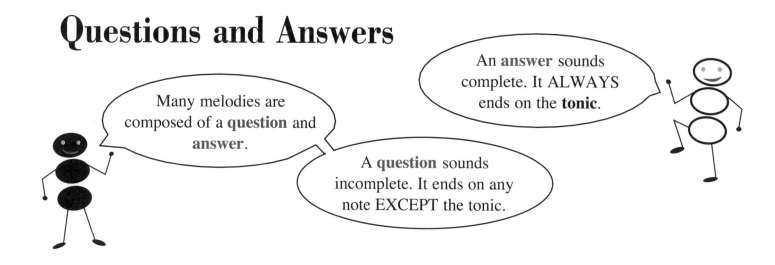

1. Play and sing the words for this **A 5-finger melody**.

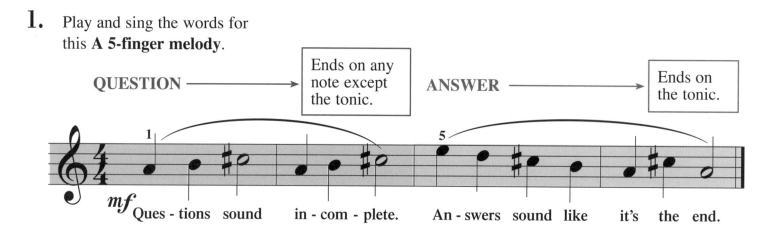

2. • Your teacher will play and say the Question.
     You improvise an **Answer** with the rhythm shown.

   • Write your favorite **Answer** on the staff. ✏️   ANSWER (Remember to include a phrase mark.)

3. • Now improvise several Questions with the rhythm shown.
     End on any note EXCEPT the tonic.

   • Write your favorite Question on the staff. ✏️

You Can Compose!

4. Complete this music using Questions and Answers.

- Choose your notes from the **A 5-finger scale**. Use the rhythm shown.
- Complete your piece by drawing a **phrase mark** over the Question, and then over the Answer.
- Play your composition!

Playing on a Cloud
A 5-Finger Scale

Words by
Crystal Bowman

QUESTION

ANSWER

rhythm:

End on the tonic!

R.H.

mf Don't you wish you could jump so high? Fly high up to the sky!

QUESTION

ANSWER

End on the tonic!

L.H.

Turn a cart-wheel and spin a-round. You would nev - er touch the ground.

QUESTION

ANSWER

End on the tonic!

R.H.

f You could leap from cloud to cloud. How you'd laugh and shout out loud!

Remember, to **improvise** means to create "on the spot."

Improvise "whirling leaves" music by doing the following:

- First, listen to your teacher play the accompaniment.
  Feel the swirling motion of the music.

- With your R.H., begin playing notes from the **A 5-finger scale** IN ANY ORDER.
  Start with a very L-O-N-G note, then another L-O-N-G note.
  Gradually let your fingers move more quickly to other notes in the scale.

- To end, fade with the teacher duet.

Whirling Leaves Improv

Teacher Improv Accompaniment: (Student improvises higher on the keyboard)

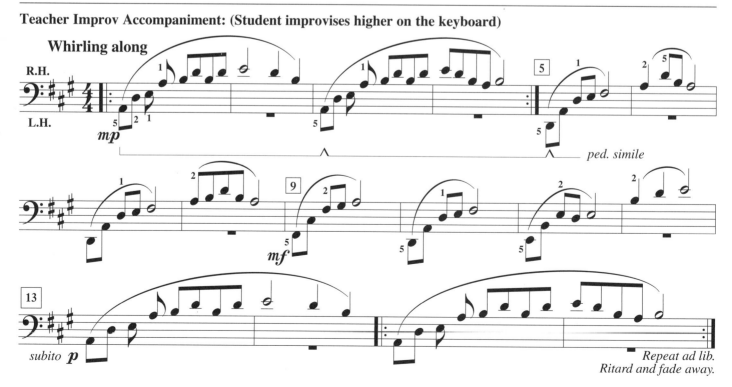

Repeat ad lib.
Ritard and fade away.

Lesson p.46 (Whirling Leaves)

Name the **chords** below. Hint: Look at the *bottom* note.

Then name aloud the 3 chord tones. Hint: Go from the lowest to the highest note.

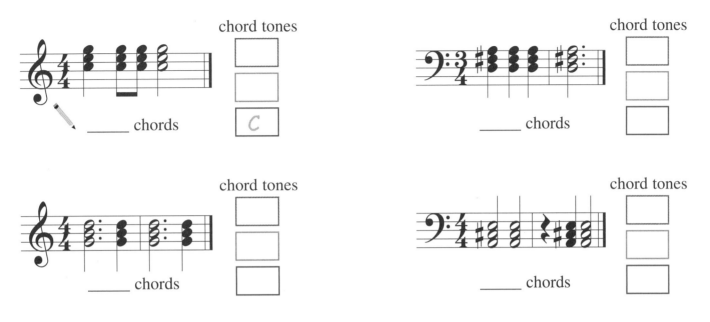

chord tones

_____ chords

| C |

chord tones

_____ chords

chord tones

_____ chords

chord tones

_____ chords

Listen to the melody your teacher plays. Does it end on the **tonic** or **dominant**?
Circle the red or blue leaf for each example.

Hint: **Tonic** sounds like the end. **Dominant** sounds incomplete.

(circle one)

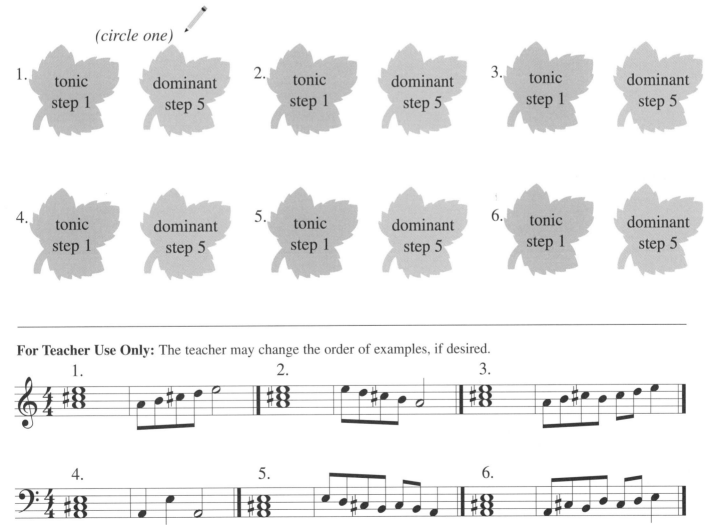

1. tonic
    step 1   dominant
                step 5

2. tonic
    step 1   dominant
                step 5

3. tonic
    step 1   dominant
                step 5

4. tonic
    step 1   dominant
                step 5

5. tonic
    step 1   dominant
                step 5

6. tonic
    step 1   dominant
                step 5

For Teacher Use Only: The teacher may change the order of examples, if desired.

1.   2.   3.

4.   5.   6.

Major and Minor Sounds

The major 5-finger scale has this pattern:

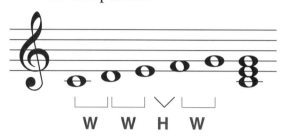

W   W   H   W

The minor 5-finger scale has the **3rd note** lowered a *half step*. It has this pattern:

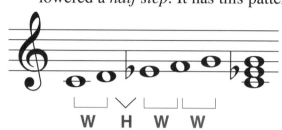

W   H   W   W

Changing Weather

1. • Circle the correct symbol for each example. MAJOR is ☀ and MINOR is ☁.
   • Then write **major** or **minor** in the blank below.

a.
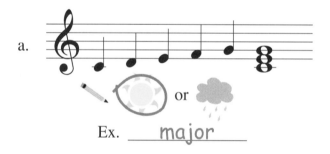

Ex. ___major___

b.
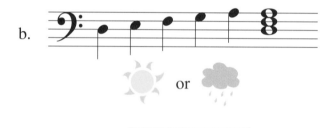

_____

c.
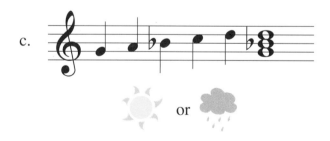

_____

d.
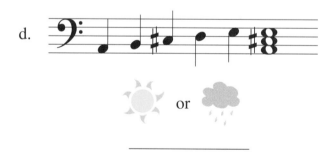

_____

e.

_____

f.
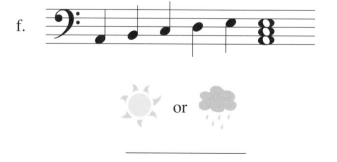

_____

Where's the Half Step?

Major Scale:
The half step is between notes **3 and 4**.

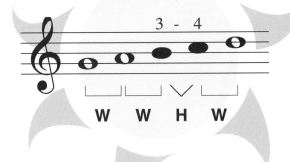

Minor Scale:
The half step is between notes **2 and 3**.

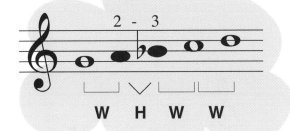

Minor Weather Change

2.
- Complete each **minor 5-finger scale**. Some scales may need flats written *in front of* the notes.
- Then mark the whole steps ⌐⌐ and half steps ∨.

C minor

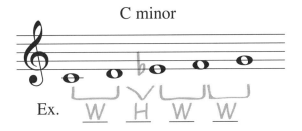

Ex.   W   H   W   W

A minor

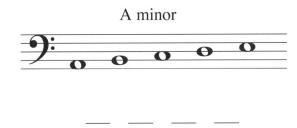

___ ___ ___ ___

C minor

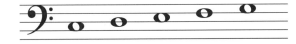

___ ___ ___ ___

Do you need a ♭?

G minor

___ ___ ___ ___

3.
- Now write your own minor 5-finger scales. Add flats, if needed.
- Mark the **whole steps** ⌐⌐ and **half steps** ∨.

D minor

C minor

G minor

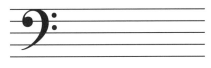

🔖 Lesson p.48 (Changing Moods)

Concert at the Old Castle

Each of these famous melodies is either **major** or **minor**.
Play and listen, then circle the answer.

Hint: If you are not sure, play the **major** and **minor**
5-finger scale to help you decide.

 Beethoven's *5th Symphony*
C 5-Finger Scale

major or **minor**
(circle one)

 Minuet from The Anna Magdalena Bach Notebook
G 5-Finger Scale

major or **minor**
(circle one)

 Mahler's *Symphony No. 1* (Frère Jacques theme)
D 5-Finger Scale

major or **minor**
(circle one)

 Haydn's *Surprise Symphony*
A 5-Finger Scale

major or **minor**
(circle one)

 Vivaldi's *Four Seasons (Spring)*
D 5-Finger Scale

major or **minor**
(circle one)

FF1082

- The 3 chords and their chord symbols for this lead sheet are:

  D major = D   D minor = Dm   A major = A

- Write the **chord symbols** in the boxes to complete the lead sheet.

- Play the lead sheet as you go to check your chord choice!

Lead Sheet for
Go Tell Aunt Rhody

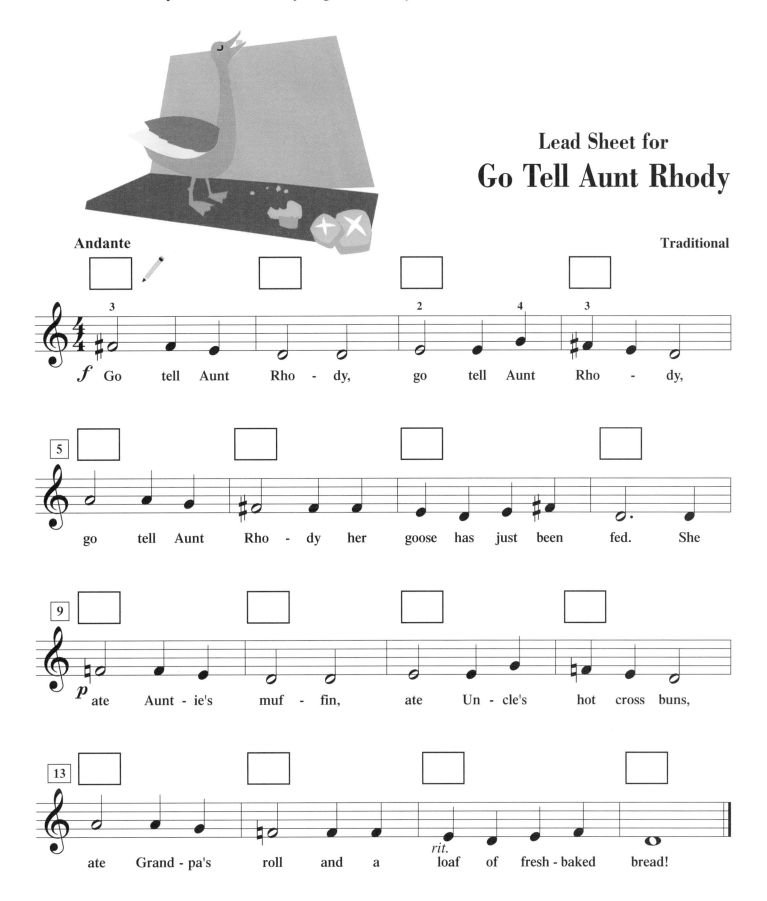

Andante   Traditional

𝆑 Go tell Aunt Rho - dy, go tell Aunt Rho - dy,

go tell Aunt Rho - dy her goose has just been fed. She

𝆏 ate Aunt - ie's muf - fin, ate Un - cle's hot cross buns,

ate Grand - pa's roll and a *rit.* loaf of fresh - baked bread!

Two bands, "The MINOR Jazz Blasts" and "The MAJOR Jazz Blasts" are competing in a Battle of the Bands contest.

Their fans are sitting in major or minor chairs.

1. Draw a line connecting each chair below to the drummer in the correct band. Hint: You may try each message on the piano to help you decide.

2. Would you like to play with The Minor Jazz Blasts or The Major Jazz Blasts?

WWHW

The third note of the scale is E♭

ABCDE

Lesson p.54 (Jazz Blast)   FF1082

BATTLE OF THE BANDS

THE MAJOR JAZZ BLASTS

Half step between 2 and 3

ABC♯DE

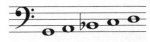

WHWW

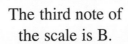

The third note of the scale is B.

Half step between 3 and 4

Congratulations! You've completed your 2A Theory Book adventure. Celebrate by creating the music for the Snake Charmer's party.

Improvise "snake charmer" music by doing the following:

- First, listen to your teacher play the accompaniment.
  Feel the mysterious mood.

- With your R.H., begin playing notes from the **G minor pattern** IN ANY ORDER.
  Notice the C♯ on finger 4 creates an exotic sound.

- To end, fade to nothing with the teacher duet.
  Then play a *forte* G minor chord together!

The Snake Charmer's Party

Teacher Improv Accompaniment: (Student improvises higher on the keyboard)